WHAT'S IT LIKE TO BE A

BABY CHIMP?

First published in the United States in 1998 by
The Millbrook Press, Inc.
2 Old New Milford Road
Brookfield, Connecticut 06804

First published in Great Britain in 1998 by
Belitha Press Limited
London House, Great Eastern Wharf
Parkgate Road, London SW11 4NQ

Editor: Honor Head
Designers: Hayley Cove, Victoria Monks
Illustrator: Matthew Nicholas
Consultants: Sally Morgan, Wendy Body

Library of Congress Cataloging-in-Publication Data
Head, Honor.
What's it like to be a baby chimp? / Honor Head ;
illustrated by Matthew Nicholas.
p. cm.
Includes index.
Summary: Describes how young chimpanzees grow
and learn to use tools, to find food, and to
communicate with other members of their group.
ISBN 0-7613-1253-6 (lib. bdg.)
1. Chimpanzees—Infancy—Juvenile literature. [1.
Chimpanzees. 2. Animals—Infancy.] I. Nicholas,
Matthew, ill. II. Title.
QL737.P96H435 1998
599.885'139—dc21 98-18268 CIP AC

Printed in Belgium

Photo credits: Ardea: pp. 26-27 (Adrian Warren, 28
(bottom) (Ferrero-Labat); BBC Natural History Unit:
pp. 11, 20 (Gerry Ellis), 15 (right) (Martha Holmes);
Bios/Still Pictures: pp. 12, 23 (Michel Gunther), 16
(J.J. Alcalay); FLPA: cover (Mark Newman), p. 15
(left) (Terry Whittaker); Getty Images: pp. 7
(Thomas Ennis), 18-19 (Manjoh Shah), 22 (Renee
Lynn); NHPA: pp. 9 (Gerard Lacz), 21 (Steve
Robinson); Photo Researcher Inc./OSF: pp. 17, 24
(Tom McHugh); Stockmarket/Zefa: pp. 13, 31;
Survival Anglia/OSF: pp. 5 (Richard Smithers),
10 (Jackie LeFevre); Woodfall Wild Images: pp. 4,
28 (top) (K. Owen).

The illustrator would like to thank Twycross Zoo,
Whipsnade Zoo, and Kew Gardens in London for
their help and advice.

WHAT'S IT LIKE TO BE A

BABY
CHIMP?

by Honor Head

Illustrated by
Matthew Nicholas

The Millbrook Press
Brookfield, Connecticut

Chimpanzees are not monkeys, but a type of ape. Apes don't have tails, and their arms are longer than their legs. They live in Africa.

Like human babies, chimpanzee babies have much to learn as they grow up. They also have a lot of fun playing games and getting into mischief.

Chimpanzees live in large, caring family groups. This book will help you to understand what it's like to be a chimp. When you read this book, imagine that you are a baby chimp. You live in a green, leafy place with lots of trees. It is hot...

When you are born you are very small and you don't have much hair. You have a pink face which will turn black as you grow older. The adult chimpanzees make a great fuss over you. They all help to look after you and enjoy playing with you.

When you grow up, your body will be covered with long, thick, black hair, except for your face, hands, and feet.

When you are very small you go everywhere with your mother. You cling to your mother's tummy all the time, even when she swings through the trees.

8

W hen you are about five months old, you learn to ride on your mother's back. As you grow bigger you sometimes slip off and have to climb back on again.

You spend about seven hours a day eating. You eat mainly fruit, seeds, and leaves.

You also like a tasty snack of ants. Termites are like big ants and they are one of your favorite foods. When you find a termite nest, you poke a stick into it. The termites cling to the stick and you lick them off.

When you feel thirsty, the whole family goes to the nearest stream or river. You drink by sucking up the water through your mouth. You make lots of slurping noises.

As you grow older you learn to use a leaf to scoop up water that is hard to reach.

You also use leaves like a sponge. You chew them until they are soft, then you soak them in water. You use the soft, wet leaves to wash yourself, or to clean a cut that is bleeding.

By the time you are one year old you can walk and climb trees. You usually walk on your hands and feet, although you can also walk upright. When you walk on all fours, you bend your fingers and walk on your knuckles.

You live on the ground and in the trees. You learn to swing from branch to branch with your long arms.

Y ou have big hands and feet. Your palms and
the soles of your feet are pink and hairless. You have
five long fingers on each hand and five long toes on
each foot.

Your fingers and toes are strong so that you can grip branches and trunks as you swing through the trees.

When it rains you don't run for shelter. Your mother sits with her head down and holds you close to her. You stay snug and dry while she gets soaking wet.

Y ou make all sorts of noises and make different faces to show other chimps how you feel. When you want to play you open your mouth wide and laugh.

When you feel scared
or angry you pull back
your lips and show
your teeth. When you
find food to eat you
bark to tell the others.

When you are excited
you shriek and scream.
You bang on trees and
slap the ground.

You have very good eyesight. Your eyes are on the front of your head, not on the sides. This is so that you can see where you are going when you swing through the trees.

You have a very short nose. You use your sense of smell to find fruit trees.

You live in a large group of chimp families. Everyone is very friendly and you give each other lots of hugs.

If you want something, you hold out your hand to ask for it.

22

Y ou say hello in many different ways. Sometimes you touch fingertips when you meet someone. Sometimes you like to kiss your friends and family and pat them on the back.

Y ou are very playful. When you are young your mother plays with you nearly all day. Playing helps you to learn how to do different things and to look after yourself.

As you grow older you begin to play with the other baby chimps. You learn to pretend fight. The adults watch over you as you play and make sure that you are safe.

You love to be groomed. Other chimps look through your hair for bits of twigs or leaves that may be caught there. Sometimes they find a small, itchy insect such as a flea.

You like to have a rest at midday when it is very hot. The family rests together.

At night your mother builds a nest high in the trees for you to sleep in. You have to be careful not to fall out during the night!

The nest is made of leaves and twigs. The branches are bent over to make a bed. It only takes ten minutes to make the nest. Your mother makes a new one every night.

If you are a girl chimp, you will spend hours helping your mother and learning to do what she does by copying her. You will have your first baby when you are about 12 years old. You will have a baby about every five years.

Both boys and girl chimps stay with the family group. You all help to look after each other. You will live for about 40 years and have many children and grandchildren.

INDEX OF USEFUL WORDS

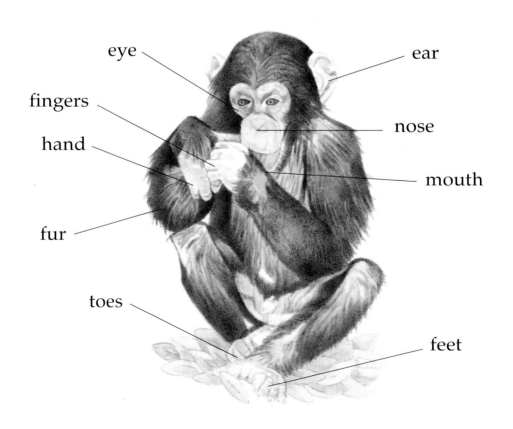

eye — ear — nose — mouth — fingers — hand — fur — toes — feet